W9-AVR-790

PHPUnit
Pocket Guide

PHPUnit
Pocket Guide

Sebastian Bergmann

O'REILLY®

Beijing · Cambridge · Farnham · Köln · Sebastopol · Tokyo

PHPUnit Pocket Guide

by Sebastian Bergmann

Copyright © 2006 O'Reilly Media, Inc. All rights reserved.
Printed in the United States of America.

Published by O'Reilly Media, Inc., 1005 Gravenstein Highway North,
Sebastopol, CA 95472.

O'Reilly books may be purchased for educational, business, or sales
promotional use. Online editions are also available for most titles
(*safari.oreilly.com*). For more information, contact our corporate/
institutional sales department: (800) 998-9938 or *corporate@oreilly.com*.

Editor:	Allison Randal
Production Editor:	Marlowe Shaeffer
Cover Designer:	Karen Montgomery
Interior Designer:	David Futato

Printing History:

October 2005:	First Edition.

Nutshell Handbook, the Nutshell Handbook logo, and the O'Reilly logo are
registered trademarks of O'Reilly Media, Inc. The *Pocket Guide* series
designations, *PHPUnit Pocket Guide*, the image of a minivet, and related
trade dress are trademarks of O'Reilly Media, Inc.

Many of the designations used by manufacturers and sellers to distinguish
their products are claimed as trademarks. Where those designations appear
in this book, and O'Reilly Media, Inc. was aware of a trademark claim, the
designations have been printed in caps or initial caps.

While every precaution has been taken in the preparation of this book, the
publisher and author assume no responsibility for errors or omissions, or for
damages resulting from the use of the information contained herein.

978-0-596-10103-9
[LSI]   [2011-08-12]

Contents

PHPUnit Pocket Guide

Introduction

For a very long time, my answer to the question, "When will you write documentation for PHPUnit?" has been, "You do not need documentation for PHPUnit. Just read the documentation for JUnit or buy a book on JUnit and adapt the code examples from Java™ and JUnit to PHP and PHPUnit." When I mentioned this to Barbara Weiss and Alexandra Follenius from the O'Reilly Germany office, they encouraged me to think it over and write a book that would serve as the documentation for PHPUnit.

Requirements

The topic of this book is PHPUnit, an open source framework for test-driven development with the PHP programming language. This book covers Version 2.3 of PHPUnit, which requires PHP 5.1. However, most of the examples should work with PHPUnit Versions 2.0–2.2, as well as PHP 5.0. The "PHPUnit for PHP 4" section, later in this book, covers the older, no longer actively developed version of PHPUnit for PHP 4.

The reader should have a good understanding of object-oriented programming with PHP 5. To German readers, I recommend my book *Professionelle Softwareentwicklung mit PHP 5* as an introduction to object-oriented programming with PHP 5. A good English book on the subject is *PHP 5 Power Programming* by Andi Gutmans, Stig Bakken, and Derick Rethans (Prentice Hall PTR).

This Book Is Free

This book is available under the Creative Commons license. You will always find the latest version of this book at its web site: *http://www.phpunit.de/pocket_guide/*. You may distribute and make changes to this book however you wish. Of course, rather than distribute your own private version of the book, I would prefer you send feedback and patches to *sb@sebastian-bergmann.de*.

Conventions Used in This Book

The following is a list of the typographical conventions used in this book:

Italic

> Indicates new terms, URLs, email addresses, filenames, file extensions, pathnames, directories, and Unix utilities.

Constant width

> Indicates commands, options, switches, variables, functions, classes, namespaces, methods, modules, parameters, values, objects, the contents of files, or the output from commands.

Constant width bold

> Shows commands or other text that should be typed literally by the user.

Constant width italic

> Shows text that should be replaced with user-supplied values.

You should pay special attention to notes set apart from the text with the following styles:

TIP

This is a tip, suggestion, or general note. It contains useful supplementary information about the topic at hand.

WARNING

This is a warning or note of caution.

How to Contact Us

We have tested and verified the information in this book to the best of our ability, but you may find that features have changed (or even that we have made mistakes!).

As a reader of this book, you can help us to improve future editions by sending us your feedback. Please let us know about any errors, inaccuracies, bugs, misleading or confusing statements, and typos that you find anywhere in this book.

Please also let us know what we can do to make this book more useful to you. We take your comments seriously and will try to incorporate reasonable suggestions into future editions. You can write to us at:

O'Reilly Media, Inc.
1005 Gravenstein Highway North
Sebastopol, CA 95472
(800) 998-9938 (in the U.S. or Canada)
(707) 829-0515 (international/local)
(707) 829-0104 (fax)

To ask technical questions or to comment on the book, send email to:

bookquestions@oreilly.com

The web site for *PHPUnit Pocket Guide* lists examples, errata, and plans for future editions. You can find this page at:

http://www.oreilly.com/catalog/phpunitpg

For more information about this book and others, see the O'Reilly web site:

http://www.oreilly.com

Acknowledgments

I would like to thank Kent Beck and Erich Gamma for JUnit and for the inspiration to write PHPUnit. I would also like to thank Kent Beck for his *JUnit Pocket Guide,* which sparked the idea for this book. I would like to thank Allison Randal, Alexandra Follenius, and Barbara Weiss for sponsoring this book at O'Reilly.

I would like to thank Andi Gutmans, Zeev Suraski, and Marcus Börger for their work on the Zend Engine 2, the core of PHP 5. I would like to thank Derick Rethans for Xdebug, the PHP extension that makes PHPUnit's code-coverage functionality possible. Finally, I would like to thank Michiel Rook, who wrote the PHPUnit tasks for Phing.

Automating Tests

Even good programmers make mistakes. The difference between a good programmer and a bad programmer is that the good programmer uses tests to detect his mistakes as soon as possible. The sooner you test for a mistake, the greater your chance of finding it, and the less it will cost to find and fix. This explains why it is so problematic to leave testing until just before releasing software. Most errors do not get caught at all, and the cost of fixing the ones you do catch is so high that you have to perform triage with the errors because you just cannot afford to fix them all.

Testing with PHPUnit is not a totally different activity from what you should already be doing. It is just a different way of doing it. The difference is between *testing*—that is, checking that your program behaves as expected—and *performing a battery of tests*—runnable code-fragments that automatically test the correctness of parts (units) of the software. These runnable code-fragments are called unit tests.

In this section, we will go from simple print-based testing code to a fully automated test. Imagine that we have been asked to test PHP's built-in Array. One bit of functionality to test is the function sizeof( ). For a newly created array, we expect the sizeof( ) function to return 0. After we add an element, sizeof( ) should return 1. Example 1 shows what we want to test.

Example 1. Testing Array and sizeof( )

```php
<?php
$fixture = Array();
// $fixture is expected to be empty.

$fixture[] = "element";
// $fixture is expected to contain one element.
?>
```

A really simple way to check whether we are getting the results we expect is to print the result of sizeof( ) before and after adding the element (see Example 2). If we get 0 and then 1, Array and sizeof( ) are behaving as expected.

Example 2. Using print to test Array and sizeof( )

```php
<?php
$fixture = Array();
print sizeof($fixture) . "\n";

$fixture[] = "element";
print sizeof($fixture) . "\n";
?>
0
1
```

Now, we would like to move from tests that require manual interpretation to tests that can run automatically. In Example 3, we write the comparison of the expected and actual values into the test code and print ok if the values are equal. If we see a not ok message, we know something is wrong.

Example 3. Comparing expected and actual values to test Array and sizeof()

```php
<?php
$fixture = Array();
print sizeof($fixture) == 0 ? "ok\n" : "not ok\n";

$fixture[] = "element";
print sizeof($fixture) == 1 ? "ok\n" : "not ok\n";
?>
ok
ok
```

We now factor out the comparison of expected and actual values into a function that raises an exception when there is a discrepancy (Example 4). Now our test output gets simpler. Nothing gets printed if the test succeeds. If we see an unhandled exception, we know something has gone wrong.

Example 4. Using an assertion function to test Array and sizeof()

```php
<?php
$fixture = Array();
assertTrue(sizeof($fixture) == 0);

$fixture[] = "element";
assertTrue(sizeof($fixture) == 1);

function assertTrue($condition) {
  if (!$condition) {
    throw new Exception("Assertion failed.");
  }
}
?>
```

The test is now completely automated. Instead of just *testing* as we did with our first version, with this version, we have an *automated test*.

The goal of using automated tests is to make fewer mistakes. While your code will still not be perfect, even with excellent tests, you will likely see a dramatic reduction in defects once you start automating tests. Automated tests give you justified confidence in your code. You can use this confidence to take more daring leaps in design (see "Refactoring," later in this book), get along better with your teammates (see "Cross-Team Tests," later in this book), improve relations with your customers, and go home every night with proof that the system is better now than it was that morning because of your efforts.

PHPUnit's Goals

So far, we only have two tests for the Array built-in and the sizeof( ) function. When we start to test the numerous array_*( ) functions PHP offers, we will need to write a test for each of them. We could write all these tests from scratch. However, it is much better to write a testing infrastructure once and then write only the unique parts of each test. PHPUnit is such an infrastructure.

Example 5 shows how we have to rewrite our two tests from Example 4 so that we can use them with PHPUnit.

Example 5. Testing Array and sizeof( ) with PHPUnit

```
<?php
require_once 'PHPUnit2/Framework/TestCase.php';

class ArrayTest extends PHPUnit2_Framework_TestCase {
    public function testNewArrayIsEmpty( ) {
        // Create the Array fixture.
        $fixture = Array( );
```

Example 5. Testing Array and sizeof() with PHPUnit (continued)

```
        // Assert that the size of the Array fixture is 0.
        $this->assertEquals(0, sizeof($fixture));
    }

    public function testArrayContainsAnElement() {
        // Create the Array fixture.
        $fixture = Array();

        // Add an element to the Array fixture.
        $fixture[] = 'Element';

        // Assert that the size of the Array fixture is 1.
        $this->assertEquals(1, sizeof($fixture));
    }
}
?>
```

Example 5 shows the basic steps for writing tests with PHPUnit:

1. The tests for a class Class go into a class ClassTest.

2. ClassTest inherits (most of the time) from PHPUnit2_Framework_TestCase.

3. The tests are public methods that expect no parameters and are named test*.

4. Inside the test methods, assertion methods such as assertEquals() (see Table 6) are used to assert that an actual value matches an expected value.

A framework such as PHPUnit has to resolve a set of constraints, some of which seem to conflict with each other. Simultaneously, tests should be:

Easy to learn to write. Tests should be easy to learn to write; otherwise, developers will not learn to write them.

Easy to write. Tests should be easy to write; otherwise, developers will not write them.

Easy to read. Test code should contain no extraneous over-head so that the test itself does not get lost in the noise that surrounds it.

Easy to execute. Tests should run at the touch of a button and present their results in a clear and unambiguous format.

Quick to execute. Tests should run fast so they can be run hundreds or thousands of times a day.

Isolated. Tests should not affect each other. If the order in which the tests are run changes, the results of the tests should not change.

Composable. We should be able to run any number or combination of tests together. This is a corollary of isolation.

There are two main clashes within this group of constraints:

Easy to learn to write versus easy to write. Tests do not generally require all the flexibility of a programming language. Many testing tools provide their own scripting language that includes only the minimum necessary features for writing tests. The resulting tests are easy to read and write because they have no noise to distract you from the content of the tests. However, learning yet another programming language and set of programming tools is inconvenient and clutters the mind.

Isolated versus quick to execute. If you want the results of one test not to affect the results of another test, each test should create the full state of the testing before it begins to execute, and return the world to its original state when it finishes. However, setting it up can take a long time (e.g., connecting to a database and initializing it to a known state using realistic data).

PHPUnit attempts to resolve these conflicts by using PHP as the testing language. Sometimes the full power of PHP is overkill for writing short, straight-line tests, but by using

PHP, we leverage all the experience and tools programmers already have in place. Because we are trying to convince reluctant testers, lowering the barrier to writing those initial tests is particularly important.

PHPUnit errs on the side of isolation over quick execution. Isolated tests are valuable because they provide high-quality feedback. You do not get a report with a bunch of test failures that were really caused because one test at the beginning of the suite failed and left the world messed up for the rest of the tests. This orientation toward isolated tests encourages designs with a large number of simple objects. Each object can be tested quickly in isolation. The result is better designs *and* faster tests.

PHPUnit assumes that most tests succeed, and it is not worth reporting the details of successful tests. When a test fails, that fact is worth noting and reporting. The vast majority of tests should succeed and are not worth commenting on, except to count the number of tests that run. This is an assumption that is really built into the reporting classes and not into the core of PHPUnit. When the results of a test run are reported, you see how many tests were executed, but you only see details for those that failed.

Tests are expected to be fine-grained, testing one aspect of one object. Hence, the first time a test fails, execution of the test halts, and PHPUnit reports the failure. It is an art to test by running many small tests. Fine-grained tests improve the overall design of the system.

When you test an object with PHPUnit, you do so only through the object's public interface. Testing based only on publicly visible behavior encourages you to confront and solve difficult design problems before the results of poor design can affect large parts of the system.

Installing PHPUnit

PHPUnit[*] is available from the PHP Extension and Application Repository (PEAR),[†] which is a framework and distribution system for reusable PHP components. It can be installed using the PEAR Installer:

```
$ pear install PHPUnit2
```

Due to PEAR's version-naming standard, the PHPUnit package for PHP 5 is called *PHPUnit2*. *PHPUnit* is the name of the PHPUnit package for PHP 4 that is the topic of "PHPUnit for PHP 4," later in this book.

After the installation, you can find the PHPUnit source files inside your local PEAR directory; the path is usually */usr/lib/php/PHPUnit2*.

Although using the PEAR installer is the only supported way to install PHPUnit, you can install PHPUnit manually. For manual installation, do the following:

1. Download a release archive from *http://pear.php.net/package/PHPUnit2/download* and extract it to a directory that is listed in the `include_path` of your *php.ini* configuration file.

2. Prepare the *phpunit* script:

   a. Rename the *pear-phpunit* script to *phpunit*.

   b. Replace the `@php_bin@` string in it with the path to your PHP command-line interpreter (usually */usr/bin/php*).

   c. Copy it to a directory that is in your *PATH* and make it executable (`chmod +x phpunit`).

3. Replace the `@package_version@` string in the *PHPUnit2/Runner/Version.php* script with the version number of the PHPUnit release you are installing (`2.3.0`, for instance).

---

[*] *http://www.phpunit.de/*

[†] *http://pear.php.net/*

The Command-Line Test Runner

The PHPUnit command-line test runner is invoked through the *phpunit* command. The following code shows how to run tests with the PHPUnit command-line test runner:

```
phpunit ArrayTest
PHPUnit 2.3.0 by Sebastian Bergmann.

..

Time: 0.067288

OK (2 tests)
```

For each test run, the PHPUnit command-line tool prints one character to indicate progress:

.   Printed when the test succeeds.

F   Printed when an assertion fails while running the test method.

E   Printed when an error occurs while running the test method.

I   Printed when the test is marked as being incomplete or not yet implemented (see "Incomplete Tests," later in this book).

PHPUnit distinguishes between *failures* and *errors*. A failure is a violated PHPUnit assertion. An error is an unexpected exception or a PHP error. Sometimes this distinction proves useful because errors tend to be easier to fix than failures. If you have a big list of problems, it's best to tackle the errors first and see if you have any failures left when the errors are all fixed.

Let's take a look at the command-line test runner's switches in the following code:

phpunit --help
PHPUnit 2.3.0 by Sebastian Bergmann.

```
Usage: phpunit [switches] UnitTest [UnitTest.php]
  --coverage-data <file> Write code-coverage data in raw
                         format to file.

  --coverage-html <file> Write code-coverage data in HTML
                         format to file.

  --coverage-text <file> Write code-coverage data in text
                         format to file.

  --testdox-html <file>  Write agile documentation in HTML
                         format to file.

  --testdox-text <file>  Write agile documentation in Text
                         format to file.

  --log-xml <file>       Log test progress in XML format
                         to file.

  --loader <loader>      TestSuiteLoader implementation to
                         use.

  --skeleton             Generate skeleton UnitTest class
                         for Unit in Unit.php.

  --wait                 Waits for a keystroke after each
                         test.

  --help                 Prints this usage information.

  --version              Prints the version and exits.
```

phpunit UnitTest

Runs the tests that are provided by the class UnitTest. This class is expected to be declared in the *UnitTest.php* source file.

UnitTest must be either a class that inherits from PHPUnit2_Framework_TestCase or a class that provides a public static suite( ) method that returns a PHPUnit2_Framework_Test object (for example, an instance of the PHPUnit2_Framework_TestSuite class).

```
phpunit UnitTest UnitTest.php
```
Runs the tests that are provided by the class `UnitTest`. This class is expected to be declared in the specified source file.

`--coverage-data`, `--coverage-html`, *and* `--coverage-text`

Controls the collection and analysis of code-coverage information for the tests that are run. (See the section "Code-Coverage Analysis," later in this book.)

`--testdox-html` *and* `--testdox-text`

Generates agile documentation in HTML or plain text format for the tests that are run. (See "Other Uses for Tests," later in this book.)

`--log-xml`

Generates a logfile in XML format for the tests run.

The following example shows the XML logfile generated for the tests in `ArrayTest`:

```xml
<?xml version="1.0" encoding="UTF-8"?>
<testsuites>
  <testsuite name="ArrayTest" tests="2" failures="0"
   errors="0" time="0.020026">
    <testcase name="testNewArrayIsEmpty"
     class="ArrayTest" time="0.014449"/>
    <testcase name="testArrayContainsAnElement"
     class="ArrayTest" time="0.005577"/>
  </testsuite>
</testsuites>
```

The following XML logfile was generated for two tests, `testFailure` and `testError`, of a test-case class named `FailureErrorTest`. It shows how failures and errors are denoted.

```xml
<?xml version="1.0" encoding="UTF-8"?>
<testsuites>
  <testsuite name="FailureErrorTest" tests="2"
failures="1" errors="1" time="0.013603">
    <testcase name="testFailure"
class="FailureErrorTest" time="0.011872">
```

```
        <failure message=""
         type="PHPUnit2_Framework_AssertionFailedError">
         </failure>
      </testcase>
      <testcase name="testError"
       class="FailureErrorTest" time="0.001731">
         <error message="" type="Exception"></error>
      </testcase>
    </testsuite>
  </testsuites>
```

--loader

> Specifies the PHPUnit2_Runner_TestSuiteLoader implementation to use.
>
> The standard test-suite loader will look for the source file in the current working directory and in each directory that is specified in PHP's include_path configuration directive. Following the PEAR Naming Conventions, a class name such as Project_Package_Class is mapped to the source file name *Project/Package/Class.php*.

--skeleton

> Generates a skeleton test-case class UnitTest (in *UnitTest. php*) for a class Unit (in *Unit.php*). For each method in the original class, there will be an incomplete test case (see "Incomplete Tests," later in this book) in the generated test-case class.
>
> The following example shows how to generate a skeleton test class for a class named Sample:
>
> **phpunit --skeleton Sample**
> PHPUnit 2.3.0 by Sebastian Bergmann.
>
> Wrote test class skeleton for Sample to SampleTest.php.
>
> **phpunit SampleTest**
> PHPUnit 2.3.0 by Sebastian Bergmann.
>
> I

```
Time: 0.007268
There was 1 incomplete test case:
1) testSampleMethod(SampleTest)


OK, but incomplete test cases!!!
Tests run: 1, incomplete test cases: 1.
```

When you are writing tests for existing code, you have to write the same code fragments over and over again, as in the following example:

```php
public function testSampleMethod() {
}
```

PHPUnit can help you by analyzing the existing code and generating a skeleton test-case class for it.

--wait

Waits for a keystroke after each test. This is useful if you are running the tests in a window that stays open only as long as the test runner is active.

TIP

When the tested code contains PHP syntax errors, the TextUI test runner might exit without printing error information. The standard test-suite loader will check the test-suite source file for PHP syntax errors, but it won't check source files included by the test-suite source file. Future versions of PHPUnit will solve this issue by using a sandboxed PHP interpreter.

Fixtures

One of the most time consuming parts of writing tests is writing the code to set up the world in a known state and then return it to its original state when the test is complete. The known state is called the *fixture* of the test.

In Example 5, the fixture was simply an array stored in the $fixture variable. Most of the time, though, the fixture will be more complex than a simple array, and the amount of code needed to set it up will grow accordingly. The actual content of the test gets lost in the noise of setting up the fixture. This problem gets even worse when you write several tests with similar fixtures. Without some help from the testing framework, we would have to duplicate the code that sets up the fixture for each test we write.

PHPUnit supports sharing the setup code. Before a test method is run, a template method called setUp( ) is invoked. setUp( ) is where you create the objects against which you will test. Once the test method has finished running, whether it succeeded or failed, another template method called tearDown( ) is invoked. tearDown( ) is where you clean up the objects against which you tested.

We can now refactor Example 5 and use setUp( ) to eliminate the code duplication that we had before. First, we declare the instance variable, $fixture, that we are going to use instead of a method-local variable. Then, we put the creation of the Array fixture into the setUp( ) method. Finally, we remove the redundant code from the test methods and use the newly introduced instance variable, $this->fixture, instead of the method-local variable $fixture with the assertEquals( ) assertion method.

```php
<?php
require_once 'PHPUnit2/Framework/TestCase.php';

class ArrayTest extends PHPUnit2_Framework_TestCase {
    protected $fixture;

    protected function setUp( ) {
        // Create the Array fixture.
        $this->fixture = Array( );
    }
```

```php
        public function testNewArrayIsEmpty() {
            // Assert that the size of the Array fixture is 0.
            $this->assertEquals(0, sizeof($this->fixture));
        }

        public function testArrayContainsAnElement() {
            // Add an element to the Array fixture.
            $this->fixture[] = 'Element';

            // Assert that the size of the Array fixture is 1.
            $this->assertEquals(1, sizeof($this->fixture));
        }
    }
    ?>
```

setUp( ) and tearDown( ) will be called once for each test method run. Although it might seem frugal to run the set up and tear down code only once for all the test methods in a test-case class, doing so would make it hard to write tests that are completely independent of each other.

Not only are setUp( ) and tearDown( ) run once for each test method, but the test methods are run in fresh instances of the test-case class (see "PHPUnit's Implementation," later in this book).

More setUp( ) than tearDown( )

setUp( ) and tearDown( ) are nicely symmetrical in theory but not in practice. In practice, you only need to implement tearDown( ) if you have allocated external resources such as files or sockets in setUp( ). If your setUp( ) just creates plain PHP objects, you can generally ignore tearDown( ). However, if you create many objects in your setUp( ), you might want to unset( ) the variables pointing to those objects in your tearDown( ) so they can be garbage collected. The garbage collection of test-case objects is not predictable.

Variations

What happens when you have two tests with slightly different setups? There are two possibilities:

- If the setUp( ) code differs only slightly, move the code
  that differs from the setUp( ) code to the test method.
- If you really have a different setUp( ), you need a different test-case class. Name the class after the difference in
  the setup.

Suite-Level Setup

PHPUnit does not provide convenient support for suite-level
setup. There aren't many good reasons to share fixtures
between tests, but, in most cases, the need to do so stems
from an unresolved design problem.

A good example of a fixture that makes sense to share across
several tests is a database connection: you log into the database once and reuse the database connection instead of creating a new connection for each test. This makes your tests run
faster. To do this, write your database tests in a test-case
class named DatabaseTests, and wrap the test suite in a
TestSetup decorator object that overrides setUp( ) to open
the database connection and tearDown( ) to close the connection, as shown in Example 6. You can run the tests from
DatabaseTests through the DatabaseTestSetup decorator by
invoking, for instance, PHPUnit's command-line test runner
with phpunit DatabaseTestSetup.

Example 6. Writing a suite-level setup decorator

```php
<?php
require_once 'PHPUnit2/Framework/TestSuite.php';
require_once 'PHPUnit2/Extensions/TestSetup.php';

class DatabaseTestSetup extends PHPUnit2_Extensions_TestSetup
{
    protected $connection = NULL;
```

Example 6. Writing a suite-level setup decorator (continued)

```
    protected function setUp() {
        $this->connection = new PDO(
            'mysql:host=wopr;dbname=test',
            'root',
            ''
        );
    }

    protected function tearDown() {
        $this->connection = NULL;
    }

    public static function suite() {
        return new DatabaseTestSetup(
            new PHPUnit2_Framework_TestSuite('DatabaseTests')
        );
    }
}
?>
```

It cannot be emphasized enough that sharing fixtures between tests reduces the value of the tests. The underlying design problem is that objects are too closely bound together. You will achieve better results by solving the underlying design problem and then writing tests using stubs (see the section "Stubs," later in this book), than by creating dependencies between tests at runtime and ignoring the opportunity to improve your design.

Testing Exceptions and Performance Regressions

PHPUnit provides two extensions that aid in the writing of tests for exceptions and performance regressions to the standard base class for test classes, PHPUnit2_Framework_TestCase.

Exceptions

How do you test exceptions? You cannot assert directly that they are raised. Instead, you have to use PHP's exception-handling facilities to write the test. The following example demonstrates testing exceptions:

```php
<?php
require_once 'PHPUnit2/Framework/TestCase.php';

class ExceptionTest extends PHPUnit2_Framework_TestCase {
    public function testException() {
        try {
            // ... Code that is expected to raise an
            //     Exception ...
            $this->fail('No Exception has been raised.');
        }

        catch (Exception $expected) {
        }
    }
}
?>
```

If the code that is expected to raise an exception does not raise an exception, the subsequent call to fail() (see Table 7, later in this book) will halt the test and signal a problem with the test. If the expected exception is raised, the catch block will be executed, and the test will continue executing.

Alternatively, you can extend your test class from PHPUnit2_Extensions_ExceptionTestCase to test whether an exception is thrown inside the tested code. Example 7 shows how to subclass PHPUnit2_Extensions_ExceptionTestCase and use its setExpectedException() method to set the expected exception. If this expected exception is not thrown, the test will be counted as a failure.

Example 7. Using PHPUnit2_Extensions_ExceptionTestCase

```php
<?php
require_once 'PHPUnit2/Extensions/ExceptionTestCase.php';

class ExceptionTest extends PHPUnit2_Extensions_
ExceptionTestCase {
    public function testException() {
        $this->setExpectedException('Exception');
    }
}
?>
```

phpunit ExceptionTest
PHPUnit 2.3.0 by Sebastian Bergmann.

F

Time: 0.006798
There was 1 failure:
1) testException(ExceptionTest)
Expected exception Exception

FAILURES!!!
Tests run: 1, Failures: 1, Errors: 0, Incomplete Tests: 0.

Table 1 shows the external protocol implemented by PHPUnit2_Extensions_ExceptionTestCase.

Table 1. Extension TestCase external protocols

Method	Description
void setExpectedException(String $exceptionName)	Sets the name of the expected exception to $exceptionName.
String getExpectedException()	Returns the name of the expected exception.

Performance Regressions

You can extend your test class from PHPUnit2_Extensions_ PerformanceTestCase to test whether the execution of a function or a method call, for instance, exceeds a specified time limit.

Example 8 shows how to subclass PHPUnit2_Extensions_ PerformanceTestCase and use its setMaxRunningTime( ) method to set the maximum running time for the test. If the test is not executed within this time limit, it will be counted as a failure.

Example 8. Using PHPUnit2_Extensions_PerformanceTestCase

```php
<?php
require_once 'PHPUnit2/Extensions/PerformanceTestCase.php';

class PerformanceTest extends PHPUnit2_Extensions_
PerformanceTestCase {
    public function testPerformance() {
        $this->setMaxRunningTime(2);
        sleep(1);
    }
}
?>
```

Table 2 shows the external protocol implemented by PHPUnit2_Extensions_PerformanceTestCase.

Table 2. Performance TestCase external protocols

Method	Description
void setMaxRunningTime(integer $maxRunningTime)	Sets the maximum running time for the test to $maxRunningTime (in seconds).
integer getMaxRunningTime( )	Returns the maximum running time allowed for the test.

Incomplete Tests

When you are working on a new test-case class, you might want to begin by writing empty test methods, such as:

```
public function testSomething() {
}
```

to keep track of the tests that you have to write. The problem with empty test methods is that they are interpreted as a success by the PHPUnit framework. This misinterpretation leads to the test reports being useless—you cannot see whether a test is actually successful or just not yet implemented. Calling $this->fail() in the unimplemented test method does not help either because then the test will be interpreted as a failure. This would be just as wrong as interpreting an unimplemented test as a success.

If we think of a successful test as a green light, and a test failure as a red light, we need an additional yellow light to mark a test as being incomplete or not yet implemented. PHPUnit2_Framework_IncompleteTest is a marker interface for marking an exception that is raised by a test method as the result of the test being incomplete or not currently implemented. PHPUnit2_Framework_IncompleteTestError is the standard implementation of this interface.

Example 9 shows a test-case class, SampleTest, that contains one test method, testSomething(). By raising the PHPUnit2_Framework_IncompleteTestError exception in the test method, we mark the test as being incomplete.

Example 9. Marking a test as incomplete

```
<?php
require_once 'PHPUnit2/Framework/TestCase.php';
require_once 'PHPUnit2/Framework/IncompleteTestError.php';

class SampleTest extends PHPUnit2_Framework_TestCase {
    public function testSomething() {
        // Optional: Test anything here, if you want.
        $this->assertTrue(TRUE, 'This should already work.');
```

Example 9. Marking a test as incomplete (continued)

```
        // Stop here and mark this test as incomplete.
        // You could use any Exception which implements the
        // PHPUnit2_Framework_IncompleteTest interface.
        throw new PHPUnit2_Framework_IncompleteTestError(
          'This test has not been implemented yet.'
        );
    }
}
?>
```

An incomplete test is denoted by an I in the output of the PHPUnit command-line test runner, as shown in the following example:

```
phpunit SampleTest
PHPUnit 2.3.0 by Sebastian Bergmann.

I

Time: 0.006657
There was 1 incomplete test case:
1) testSomething(SampleTest)
This test has not been implemented yet.

OK, but incomplete test cases!!!
Tests run: 1, incomplete test cases: 1.
```

Test-First Programming

Unit tests are a vital part of several software development practices and processes, such as test-first programming, Extreme Programming,[*] and test-driven development.[†] They also allow for design-by-contract[‡] in programming languages that do not support this methodology with language constructs.

---

[*] *http://en.wikipedia.org/wiki/Extreme_Programming*
[†] *http://en.wikipedia.org/wiki/Test-driven_development*
[‡] *http://en.wikipedia.org/wiki/Design_by_Contract*

You can use PHPUnit to write tests once you are done programming. However, the sooner a test is written after an error has been introduced, the more valuable the test is. So, instead of writing tests months after the code is "complete," we can write tests days, hours, or minutes after the possible introduction of a defect. Why stop there? Why not write the tests a little before the possible introduction of a defect?

Test-first programming, which is part of Extreme Programming and test-driven development, builds upon this idea and takes it to the extreme. With today's computational power, we have the opportunity to run thousands of tests, thousands of times per day. We can use the feedback from all of these tests to program in small steps, each of which carries with it the assurance of a new automated test, in addition to all the tests that have come before. The tests are like pitons, assuring you that no matter what happens, once you have made progress, you can only fall so far.

When you first write the test, it cannot possibly run because you are calling on objects and methods that have not been programmed yet. This might feel strange at first, but, after a while, you will get used to it. Think of test-first programming as a pragmatic approach to following the object-oriented programming principle of programming to an interface instead of programming to an implementation: while you are writing the test, you are thinking about the interface of the object you are testing—what does this object look like from the outside? When you go to make the test really work, you are thinking about pure implementation. The interface is fixed by the failing test.

What follows is a necessarily abbreviated introduction to test-first programming. You can explore the topic further in other books, such as *Test-Driven Development: By Example* by Kent Beck (Addison Wesley) or *Test-Driven Development: A Practical Guide* by Dave Astels (Prentice Hall).

BankAccount Example

In this section, we will look at the example of a class that represents a bank account. The contract for the BankAccount class requires methods to get and set the bank account's balance, as well as methods to deposit and withdraw money. It also specifies that the following two conditions must be ensured:

- The bank account's initial balance must be zero.
- The bank account's balance cannot become negative.

Following the test-first programming approach, we write the tests for the BankAccount class before we write the code for the class itself. We use the contract conditions as the basis for the tests and name the test methods accordingly, as shown in Example 10.

Example 10. Tests for the BankAccount class

```php
<?php
require_once 'PHPUnit2/Framework/TestCase.php';
require_once 'BankAccount.php';

class BankAccountTest extends PHPUnit2_Framework_TestCase {
    private $ba;

    protected function setUp() {
        $this->ba = new BankAccount;
    }

    public function testBalanceIsInitiallyZero() {
        $this->assertEquals(0, $this->ba->getBalance());
    }

    public function testBalanceCannotBecomeNegative() {
        try {
            $this->ba->withdrawMoney(1);
        }
```

Example 10. Tests for the BankAccount class (continued)

```
        catch (Exception $e) {
            return;
        }

        $this->fail();
    }

    public function testBalanceCannotBecomeNegative2() {
        try {
            $this->ba->depositMoney(-1);
        }

        catch (Exception $e) {
            return;
        }

        $this->fail();
    }

    public function testBalanceCannotBecomeNegative3() {
        try {
            $this->ba->setBalance(-1);
        }

        catch (Exception $e) {
            return;
        }

        $this->fail();
    }
}
?>
```

We now write the minimal amount of code needed for the
first test, testBalanceIsInitiallyZero( ), to pass. In our
example, this amounts to implementing the getBalance( )
method of the BankAccount class, as shown in Example 11.

Example 11. Code needed for the testBalanceIsInitiallyZero() test to pass

```php
<?php
class BankAccount {
    private $balance = 0;

    public function getBalance() {
        return $this->balance;
    }
}
?>
```

The test for the first contract condition now passes, but the tests for the second contract condition fail because we have yet to implement the methods that these tests call:

phpunit BankAccountTest
PHPUnit 2.3.0 by Sebastian Bergmann.

.
Fatal error: Call to undefined method BankAccount::
withdrawMoney()

For the tests that ensure the second contract condition to pass, we now need to implement the withdrawMoney(), depositMoney(), and setBalance() methods, as shown in Example 12. These methods are written in such a way that they raise an InvalidArgumentException when they are called with illegal values that would violate the contract conditions.

Example 12. The complete BankAccount class

```php
<?php
class BankAccount {
    private $balance = 0;

    public function getBalance() {
        return $this->balance;
    }
```

Example 12. The complete BankAccount class (continued)

```
    public function setBalance($balance) {
        if ($balance >= 0) {
            $this->balance = $balance;
        } else {
            throw new InvalidArgumentException;
        }
    }

    public function depositMoney($amount) {
        if ($amount >= 0) {
            $this->balance += $amount;
        } else {
            throw new InvalidArgumentException;
        }
    }

    public function withdrawMoney($amount) {
        if ($amount >= 0 && $this->balance >= $amount) {
            $this->balance -= $amount;
        } else {
            throw new InvalidArgumentException;
        }
    }
}
?>
```

The tests that ensure the second contract condition now pass, too:

```
phpunit BankAccountTest
PHPUnit 2.3.0 by Sebastian Bergmann.

....

Time: 0.057038

OK (4 tests)
```

Alternatively, you can use the static assertion methods provided by the PHPUnit2_Framework_Assert class to write the contract conditions as design-by-contract style assertions

---

into your code, as shown in Example 13. When one of these assertions fails, a PHPUnit2_Framework_AssertionFailedError exception will be raised. With this approach, you write less code for the contract condition checks, and the tests become more readable. However, you add a runtime dependency on PHPUnit to your project.

Example 13. The BankAccount class with design-by-contract assertions

```php
<?php
require_once 'PHPUnit2/Framework/Assert.php';

class BankAccount {
    private $balance = 0;

    public function getBalance() {
        return $this->balance;
    }

    public function setBalance($balance) {
        PHPUnit2_Framework_Assert::assertTrue($balance >= 0);

        $this->balance = $balance;
    }

    public function depositMoney($amount) {
        PHPUnit2_Framework_Assert::assertTrue($amount >= 0);

        $this->balance += $amount;
    }

    public function withdrawMoney($amount) {
        PHPUnit2_Framework_Assert::assertTrue($amount >= 0);
        PHPUnit2_Framework_Assert::assertTrue($this->balance
            >= $amount);

        $this->balance -= $amount;
    }
}
?>
```

By writing the contract conditions into the tests, we have used design-by-contract to program the BankAccount class. We then wrote, following the test-first programming approach, the code needed to make the tests pass. However, we forgot to write tests that call setBalance( ), depositMoney( ), and withdrawMoney( ) with legal values that do not violate the contract conditions. We need a means to test our tests or, at least, to measure their quality. Such a means is the analysis of code-coverage information that we will discuss next.

Code-Coverage Analysis

You have learned how to use unit tests to test your code. But how do you test your tests? How do you find code that is not yet tested—or, in other words, not yet *covered* by a test? How do you measure testing completeness? All these questions are answered by a practice called code-coverage analysis. Code-coverage analysis gives you an insight into what parts of the production code are executed when the tests are run.

PHPUnit's code-coverage analysis utilizes the statement coverage functionality provided by the Xdebug* extension. An example of what statement coverage means is that if there is a method with 100 lines of code, and only 75 of these lines are actually executed when tests are being run, then the method is considered to have a code overage of 75 percent.

Figure 1 shows a code-coverage report for the BankAccount class (from Example 12) in HTML format generated by the PHPUnit command-line test runner's --coverage-html switch. Executable code lines are black; non-executable code lines are gray. Code lines that are actually executed are highlighted.

* http://www.xdebug.org/

```php
1   <?php
2   class BankAccount {
3       private $balance=0;
4
5       public function getBalance() {
6               return $this->balance;
7       }
8
9       public function setBalance($balance) {
10              if ($balance >=0) {
11                      $this->balance=$balance
12              } else {
13                      throw new InvalidArgumentException;
14              }
15      }
16
17      public function depositMoney($amount)
18              if ($amount >=0) {
19                      $this->balance+=$amount;
20              } else {
21                      throw new InvalidArgumentException;
22              }
23 }
24
25      public function withdrawMoney($amount) {
26              if ($amount >=0 && $this->balance >= $amount) {
27                      $this->balance -=$amount;
28              } else {
29                      throw new InvalidArgumentException;
30              }
31      }
32 }
33 ?>
```

Figure 1. The BankAccount class, not completely covered by tests

The code-coverage report shows that we need to write tests that call setBalance( ), depositMoney( ), and withdrawMoney( ) with legal values in order to achieve complete code coverage. Example 14 shows tests that need to be added to the BankAccountTest test-case class to completely cover the BankAccount class.

Example 14. The BankAccount class, covered by tests

```php
<?php
require_once 'PHPUnit2/Framework/TestCase.php';
require_once 'BankAccount.php';

class BankAccountTest extends PHPUnit2_Framework_TestCase {
    // ...
```

Example 14. The BankAccount class, covered by tests (continued)

```php
    public function testSetBalance() {
        $this->ba->setBalance(1);
        $this->assertEquals(1, $this->ba->getBalance());
    }

    public function testDepositAndWidthdrawMoney() {
        $this->ba->depositMoney(1);
        $this->assertEquals(1, $this->ba->getBalance());

        $this->ba->withdrawMoney(1);
        $this->assertEquals(0, $this->ba->getBalance());
    }
}
?>
```

In Figure 2, we see that the BankAccount class is now covered completely by tests.

In the "PHPUnit and Phing" section, later in this book, you will learn how to use Phing to generate more detailed code-coverage reports.

Stubs

Tests that only test one thing are more informative than tests in which failure can come from many sources. How can you isolate your tests from external influences? Simply put, by replacing the expensive, messy, unreliable, slow, complicated resources with stubs made from plain PHP objects. For example, you can implement what is in reality a complicated computation by returning a constant, at least for the purposes of a single test.

Stubs solve the problem of allocating expensive external resources. For example, sharing a resource, such as a database connection, between tests by using the PHPUnit2_Extensions_TestSetup decorator helps, but not using the database for the purposes of the tests at all is even better.

```php
 1  <?php
 2  class BankAccount {
 3      private $balance=0;
 4
 5      public function getBalance() {
 6              return $this->balance;
 7      }
 8
 9      public function setBalance($balance) {
10              if ($balance >=0) {
11                      $this->balance=$balance
12              } else {
13                      throw new InvalidArgumentException;
14              }
15      }
16
17      public function depositMoney($amount)
18              if ($amount >=0) {
19                      $this->balance+=$amount;
20              } else {
21                      throw new InvalidArgumentException;
22              }
23  }
24
25      public function withdrawMoney($amount) {
26              if ($amount >=0 && $this->balance >= $amount) {
27                      $this->balance -=$amount;
28              } else {
29                      throw new InvalidArgumentException;
30              }
31      }
32  }
33  ?>
```

Figure 2. The BankAccount class is completely covered by tests

Design improvement is one effect of using stubs. Widely used resources are accessed through a single façade, so you can easily replace the resource with the stub. For example, instead of having direct database calls scattered throughout the code, you have a single Database object—an implementor of the IDatabase interface. Then, you can create a stub implementation of IDatabase and use it for your tests. You can even create an option for running the tests with the stub database or the real database, so you can use your tests for both local testing during development and integration testing with the real database.

Functionality that needs to be stubbed out tends to cluster in the same object, improving cohesion. By presenting the functionality with a single, coherent interface, you reduce the coupling with the rest of the system.

Self-Shunting

Sometimes you need to check that an object has been called correctly. You can create a complete stub of the object to be called, but that can make it inconvenient to check for correct results. A simpler solution is to apply the *self-shunt pattern* and use the test-case object itself as a stub. The term self-shunting is taken from the medical practice of installing a tube that takes blood from an artery and returns it to a vein to provide a convenient place for injecting drugs.

Here is an example: suppose we want to test that the correct method is called on an object that observes another object. First, we make our test-case class an implementor of Observer:

```
class ObserverTest extends PHPUnit2_Framework_TestCase
implements Observer{
}
```

Next, we implement the one Observer method, update( ), to check that it is called when the state of the observed Subject object changes:

```
public $wasCalled = FALSE;

public function update(Subject $subject) {
    $this->wasCalled = TRUE;
}
```

Now, we can write our test. We create a new Subject object and attach the test object to it as an observer. When the state of the Subject changes—for instance, by calling its doSomething( ) method—the Subject object has to call the update( ) method on all objects that are registered as observers. We use the $wasCalled instance variable that is set by our implementation of update( ) to check whether the Subject object does what it is supposed to do:

```php
public function testUpdate() {
    $subject = new Subject;
    $subject->attach($this);
    $subject->doSomething( );

    $this->assertTrue($this->wasCalled);
}
```

Notice that we create a new Subject object instead of relying on a global instance. Stubbing encourages this style of design. It reduces the coupling between objects and improves reuse.

If you are not familiar with the self-shunt pattern, the tests can be hard to read. What is going on here? Why is a test case also an observer? But once you get used to the idiom, the tests are easy to read. Everything you need to understand a test is in one class.

Other Uses for Tests

Once you get used to writing automated tests, you will likely discover more uses for tests. Here are some examples.

Agile Documentation

Typically, in a project that is developed using an agile process, such as Extreme Programming, the documentation cannot keep up with the frequent changes to the project's design and code. Extreme Programming demands *collective code ownership*, so all developers need to know how the entire system works. If you are disciplined enough to use "speaking names" for your tests that describe what a class should do, you can use PHPUnit's TestDox functionality to generate automated documentation for your project based on its tests. This documentation gives developers an overview of what each class of the project is supposed to do.

PHPUnit's TestDox functionality looks at a test class and all the test method names and converts them from camel case PHP names to sentences: `testBalanceIsInitiallyZero()` becomes "Balance is initially zero." If there are several test methods whose names differ only by a suffix of one or more digits, such as `testBalanceCannotBecomeNegative()` and `testBalanceCannotBecomeNegative2()`, the sentence "Balance cannot become negative" will appear only once, assuming that all of these tests succeed.

The following code shows the agile documentation for the Bank Account class (in Example 10) generated by running `phpunit --testdox-text BankAccountTest.txt BankAccountTest`:

```
BankAccount
 - Balance is initially zero
 - Balance cannot become negative
```

Alternatively, the agile documentation can be generated in HTML format by using `--testdox-html BankAccountTest.htm`.

Agile documentation can be used to document the assumptions you make about the external packages in your project. When you use an external package, you are exposed to the risks that the package will not behave as you expect, and that future versions of the package will change in subtle ways that will break your code, without you knowing it. You can address these risks by writing a test about how the external package works every time you make an assumption. If your test succeeds, your assumption is valid. If you document all your assumptions with tests, future releases of the external package will be no cause for concern: if the tests succeed, your system should continue working.

Cross-Team Tests

When you document assumptions with tests, you own the tests. The supplier of the package—who you make assumptions about—knows nothing about your tests. If you want a closer relationship with the supplier of a package, you can use the tests to communicate and coordinate your activities.

When you agree on coordinating your activities with the supplier of a package, you can write the tests together. Do this in such a way that the tests reveal as many assumptions as possible. Hidden assumptions are the death of cooperation. With the tests, you document exactly what you expect from the supplied package. The supplier will know the package is complete when all the tests run.

By using stubs (see the section "Stubs," earlier in this book), you can further decouple yourself from the supplier. The job of the supplier is to make the tests run with the real implementation of the package. Your job is to make the tests run for your own code. Until such time as you have the real implementation of the supplied package, you use stub objects. Following this approach, the two teams can develop independently.

Debugging Tests

When you get a defect report, your impulse might be to fix the defect as quickly as possible. Experience shows that this impulse will not serve you well; it is likely that the fix for the defect will cause another defect.

You can hold your impulse in check by doing the following:

1. Verifying that you can reproduce the defect.
2. Finding the smallest-scale demonstration of the defect in the code. For example, if a number appears incorrectly in an output, find the object that is computing that number.
3. Writing an automated test that fails but will succeed when the defect is fixed.
4. Fixing the defect.

Finding the smallest reliable reproduction of the defect gives you the opportunity to really examine the cause of the defect. The test you write will improve the chances that when you fix the defect, you really fix it, because the new test reduces the likelihood of undoing the fix with future code changes.

All the tests you wrote before reduce the likelihood of inadvertently causing a different problem.

Refactoring

Refactoring, the controlled technique for improving the design of an existing code base, can be applied safely only when you have a test suite. Otherwise, you might not notice the system breaking while you are carrying out the restructuring. Refactoring can be broken down into a series of small behavior-preserving transformations.

The following conditions will help you to improve the code and design of your project, while using unit tests to verify that the refactoring's transformation steps are, indeed, behavior- preserving and do not introduce errors:

1. All unit tests run correctly.
2. The code communicates its design principles.
3. The code contains no redundancies.
4. The code contains the minimal number of classes and methods.

PHPUnit and Phing

Phing (PHing Is Not GNU make)* is a project-build system based on Apache Ant.† In the context of PHP, you do not need to build and compile your sources; the intention of Phing is to ease the packaging, deployment, and testing of applications. For these tasks, Phing provides numerous out-of-the-box operation modules ("tasks") and an easy-to-use, object-oriented model for adding your own custom tasks.

Phing can be installed using the PEAR Installer, as shown in the following command line:

```
pear install http://phing.info/pear/phing-2.1.0-pear.tgz
```

* *http://www.phing.info/wiki/*
† *http://ant.apache.org/*

Phing uses simple XML build files that specify a target tree where various tasks are executed. One out-of-the-box task that comes with Phing is the <phpunit2> task that runs test cases using the PHPUnit framework. It is a functional port of Apache Ant's JUnit task.

Example 15 shows a Phing *build.xml* file that specifies a <project> named BankAccount. The project's default <target> is called *test*. Using the <phpunit2> task, this target runs all test cases that can be found in source files that match the *Test.php condition. This is done by using a <batchtest> element that collects the included files from any number of nested <fileset> elements. In this example, the tests declared in the class BankAccountTest in the source file *BankAccountTest.php* will be run.

Example 15. Phing build.xml file for the BankAccount tests

```xml
<?xml version="1.0"?>

<project name="BankAccount" basedir="." default="test">
  <target name="test">
    <phpunit2 haltonfailure="true" printsummary="true">
      <batchtest>
        <fileset dir=".">
          <include name="*Test.php"/>
        </fileset>
      </batchtest>
    </phpunit2>
  </target>
</project>
```

Invoking Phing in the directory that contains *build.xml* (Example 15), *BankAccount.php* (Example 12), and *BankAccountTest.php* (Example 10) will run the tests by executing the project's default target, *tests*:

```
phing
Buildfile: /home/sb/build.xml

BankAccount > test:
 [phpunit2] Tests run: 4, Failures: 0, Errors: 0, Time
elapsed: 0.00067 sec
```

```
BUILD FINISHED

Total time: 0.0960 seconds
```

Table 3 shows the parameters that can be used to configure the <phpunit2> task.

Table 3. Attributes for the <phpunit2> element

Name	Type	Description	Default
haltonerror	Boolean	Stops the build process if an error occurs during the test run.	false
haltonfailure	Boolean	Stops the build process if a test fails. Errors are considered failures as well.	false
printsummary	Boolean	Prints one-line statistics for each test case.	false

The following example shows the <phpunit2> task's output when a test fails:

```
phing
Buildfile: /home/sb/build.xml

BankAccount > test:
 [phpunit2] Tests run: 4, Failures: 1, Errors: 0, Time
elapsed: 0.00067 sec
Execution of target "test" failed for the following
reason:
/home/sb/build.xml:5:37: One or more tests failed

BUILD FAILED
/home/sb/build.xml:5:37: One or more tests failed
Total time: 0.0968 seconds
```

Formatting Feedback

Besides the required <batchtest> element, the <phpunit2> element allows for another nested element: <formatter> is used to write test results in different formats. Output will always be sent to a file, unless you set the usefile attribute to false.

The name of the file is predetermined by the formatter and can be changed by the `outfile` attribute. There are three predefined formatters:

`brief`
> Prints detailed information in plain text only for test cases that failed.

`plain`
> Prints one-line statistics in plain text for all test cases.

`xml`
> Writes the test results in XML format.

Table 4 shows the parameters that can be used to configure the `<formatter>` task.

Table 4. Attributes for the <formatter> element

Name	Type	Description	Default
`type`	String	Name of a predefined formatter (xml, plain, or brief).	
`classname`	String	Name of a custom formatter class.	
`usefile`	Boolean	Flag marking whether output should be sent to a file.	`true`
`todir`	String	Directory the file is written to.	
`outfile`	String	Name of the file that is written to.	Depends on the formatter used.

To generate a test report in HTML format, you can use the `<phpunit2report>` task, which applies an XSLT stylesheet to the XML logfile created by the `<formatter>` task. Phing ships with two XSLT stylesheets—*phpunit2-frames.xsl* and *phpunit2-noframes.xsl*—that generate HTML reports with or without frames, respectively.

Example 16 shows a *build.xml* file for Phing that runs the tests from the `BankAccountTest` class and generates a test report in HTML format using the *phpunit2-frames.xsl* XSLT stylesheet. The HTML files generated for the report will be written to the *report/* directory that is created by the "prepare" `<target>` and deleted by the "clean" `<target>`.

Example 16. Applying an XSLT stylesheet to get a test report

```xml
<?xml version="1.0"?>

<project name="BankAccount" basedir="." default="report">
  <target name="prepare">
    <mkdir dir="report"/>
  </target>

  <target name="clean">
    <delete dir="report"/>
  </target>

  <target name="report" depends="prepare">
    <phpunit2>
      <batchtest>
        <fileset dir=".">
          <include name="*Test.php"/>
        </fileset>
      </batchtest>

      <formatter type="xml" todir="report"
                 outfile="logfile.xml"/>
    </phpunit2>

    <phpunit2report infile="report/logfile.xml"
                    format="frames" styledir="."
                    todir="report"/>
  </target>
</project>
```

The following example shows the output of the phing command as it runs:

```
phing
Buildfile: /home/sb/build.xml
```

```
BankAccount > prepare:
    [mkdir] Created dir: /home/sb/report

BankAccount > report:

BUILD FINISHED

Total time: 0.1112 seconds
```

Figure 3 shows the title page of the generated test report.

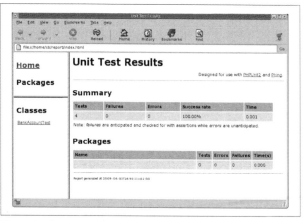

Figure 3. The generated test report

Table 5 shows the parameters that can be used to configure the <phpunit2report> task.

Table 5. Attributes for the <phpunit2report> element

Name	Type	Description	Default
infile	String	The filename of the XML results file to use.	testsuites.xml
format	String	The format of the generated report. Must be frames or noframes.	noframes

Table 5. Attributes for the <phpunit2report> element (continued)

Name	Type	Description	Default
styledir	String	The directory in which the stylesheets are located. The stylesheets must conform to the following conventions: the stylesheet for the frames format must be named *phpunit2-frames.xsl,* the stylesheet for the noframes format must be named *phpunit2-noframes.xsl.*	
todir	String	The directory to which the files resulting from the transformation should be written.	

In addition to the test report that we just generated, Phing can generate a code-coverage report. For this, we need the <coverage-setup> and <coverage-report> tasks. The former prepares a database in which code-coverage information is stored while the tests are run; the latter formats such a database into a report in HTML format using XSLT stylesheets.

Example 17 shows a *build.xml* file for Phing that runs the tests from the BankAccountTest class and generates a code-coverage report in HTML format.

Example 17. Generating a code-coverage report

```xml
<?xml version="1.0"?>

<project name="BankAccount" basedir="."
         default="coverage-report">
  <target name="prepare">
    <mkdir dir="coverage-report"/>
  </target>

  <target name="clean">
    <delete dir="coverage-report"/>
  </target>
```

Example 17. Generating a code-coverage report (continued)

```
<target name="coverage-report" depends="prepare">
  <coverage-setup database="./coverage-report/database">
    <fileset dir=".">
      <include name="*.php"/>
      <exclude name="*Test.php"/>
    </fileset>
  </coverage-setup>

  <phpunit2>
    <batchtest>
      <fileset dir=".">
        <include name="*Test.php"/>
      </fileset>
    </batchtest>
  </phpunit2>

  <coverage-report outfile="coverage-report/coverage.xml">
    <report todir="coverage-report" styledir="."/>
  </coverage-report>
</target>
</project>
```

Figure 4 shows the title page of the generated code-coverage report.

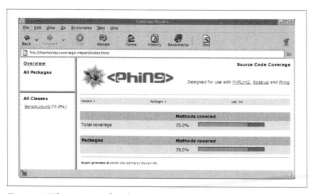

Figure 4. The generated code-coverage report

PHPUnit's Implementation

The implementation of PHPUnit is a bit unusual, using techniques that are difficult to maintain in ordinary application code. Understanding how PHPUnit runs your tests can help you write them.

A single test is represented by a `PHPUnit2_Framework_Test` object and requires a `PHPUnit2_Framework_TestResult` object to be run. The `PHPUnit2_Framework_TestResult` object is passed to the `PHPUnit2_Framework_Test` object's `run()` method, which runs the actual test method and reports any exceptions to the `PHPUnit2_Framework_TestResult` object. This is an idiom from the Smalltalk world called *Collecting Parameter*. It suggests that when you need to collect results from several methods (in our case the results of the several invocations of the `run()` method for the various tests), you should add a parameter to the method and pass an object that will collect the results for you. See the article "JUnit: A Cook's Tour" by Erich Gamma and Kent Beck (*http://junit.sourceforge.net/doc/cookstour/cookstour.htm*) and *Smalltalk Best Practice Patterns* by Kent Beck (Prentice Hall).

To further understand how PHPUnit runs your tests, consider the test-case class in Example 18.

Example 18. The EmptyTest class

```php
<?php
require_once 'PHPUnit2/Framework/TestCase.php';

class EmptyTest extends PHPUnit2_Framework_TestCase {
    private $emptyArray = array();

    public function testSize() {
        $this->assertEquals(0, sizeof($this->emptyArray));
    }

    public function testIsEmpty() {
        $this->assertTrue(empty($this->emptyArray));
    }
}
```

Example 18. The EmptyTest class (continued)

```
}
?>
```

When the test is run, the first thing PHPUnit does is convert the test class into a PHPUnit2_Framework_Test object—here, a PHPUnit2_Framework_TestSuite containing two instances of EmptyTest, as shown in Figure 5.

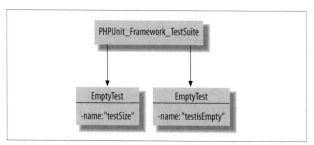

Figure 5. Tests about to be run

When the PHPUnit2_Framework_TestSuite is run, it runs each of the EmptyTests in turn. Each runs its own setUp( ) method, creating a fresh $emptyArray for each test, as shown in Figure 6. This way, if one test modifies the list, the other test will not be affected. Even changes to global and super-global (such as $_ENV) variables do not affect other tests.

In short, one test-case class results in a two-level tree of objects when the tests are run. Each test method works with its own copy of the objects created by setUp( ). The result is tests that can run completely independently.

To run the test method itself, PHPUnit uses reflection to find the method name in the instance variable $name and invokes it. This is another idiom, called *Pluggable Selector*, that is commonly used in the Smalltalk world. Using a Pluggable Selector makes writing tests simpler, but there is a tradeoff: you cannot look at the code to decide whether a method is invoked, you have to look at the data values at runtime.

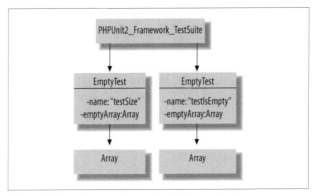

Figure 6. Tests after running, each with its own fixture

PHPUnit API

For most uses, PHPUnit has a simple API: subclass `PHPUnit2_Framework_TestCase` for your test cases and call `assertTrue()` or `assertEquals()`. However, for those of you who would like to look deeper into PHPUnit, here are all of its published methods and classes.

Overview

Most of the time, you will encounter five classes or interfaces when you are using PHPUnit:

`PHPUnit2_Framework_Assert`
  A collection of static methods for checking actual values against expected values

`PHPUnit2_Framework_Test`
  The interface of all objects that act like tests

`PHPUnit2_Framework_TestCase`
  A single test

`PHPUnit2_Framework_TestSuite`
  A collection of tests

PHPUnit2_Framework_TestResult

A summary of the results of running one or more tests

Figure 7 shows the relationship of the five basic classes and interfaces in PHPUnit: PHPUnit2_Framework_Assert, PHPUnit2_Framework_Test, PHPUnit2_Framework_TestCase, PHPUnit2_Framework_TestSuite, and PHPUnit2_Framework_TestResult.

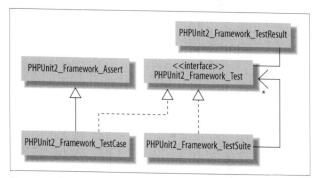

Figure 7. The five basic classes and interfaces in PHPUnit

PHPUnit2_Framework_Assert

Most test cases written for PHPUnit are derived indirectly from the class PHPUnit2_Framework_Assert, which contains methods for automatically checking values and reporting discrepancies. The methods are declared static, so you can write design-by-contract style assertions in your methods and have them reported through PHPUnit (Example 19).

Example 19. Design-by-contract style assertions

```php
<?php
require_once 'PHPUnit2/Framework/Assert.php';

class Sample {
    public function aSampleMethod($object) {
        PHPUnit2_Framework_Assert::assertNotNull($object);
    }
}
```

Example 19. Design-by-contract style assertions (continued)

```
$sample = new Sample;
$sample->aSampleMethod(NULL);
?>
Fatal error: Uncaught exception
    'PHPUnit2_Framework_AssertionFailedError'
with message 'expected: <NOT NULL> but was: <NULL>'
```

Most of the time, though, you'll be checking the assertions inside of tests.

There are two variants of each of the assertion methods: one takes a message to be displayed with the error as a parameter, and one does not. Example 20 demonstrates an assertion method with a message. The optional message is typically displayed when a failure is displayed, which can make debugging easier.

Example 20. Using assertions with messages

```
<?php
require_once 'PHPUnit2/Framework/TestCase.php';

class MessageTest extends PHPUnit2_Framework_TestCase {
    public function testMessage() {
        $this->assertTrue(FALSE, 'This is a custom message.');
    }
}
?>
```

The following example shows the output you get when you run the testMessage( ) test from Example 20, using assertions with messages:

```
phpunit MessageTest.php
PHPUnit 2.3.0 by Sebastian Bergmann.

F

Time: 0.102507
There was 1 failure:
1) testMessage(MessageTest)
This is a custom message.
```

```
FAILURES!!!
Tests run: 1, Failures: 1, Errors: 0, Incomplete Tests: 0.
```

Table 6 shows all the varieties of assertions.

Table 6. Assertions

Assertion	Description
void assertTrue(Boolean $condition)	Reports an error if $condition is FALSE.
void assertTrue(Boolean $condition, String $message)	Reports an error identified by $message if $condition is FALSE.
void assertFalse(Boolean $condition)	Reports an error if $condition is TRUE.
void assertFalse(Boolean $condition, String $message)	Reports an error identified by $message if $condition is TRUE.
void assertNull(Mixed $variable)	Reports an error if $variable is not NULL.
void assertNull(Mixed $variable, String $message)	Reports an error identified by $message if $variable is not NULL.
void assertNotNull(Mixed $variable)	Reports an error if $variable is NULL.
void assertNotNull(Mixed $variable, String $message)	Reports an error identified by $message if $variable is NULL.
void assertSame(Object $expected, Object $actual)	Reports an error if the two variables $expected and $actual do not reference the same object.
void assertSame(Object $expected, Object $actual, String $message)	Reports an error identified by $message if the two variables $expected and $actual do not reference the same object.
void assertSame(Mixed $expected, Mixed $actual)	Reports an error if the two variables $expected and $actual do not have the same type and value.
void assertSame(Mixed $expected, Mixed $actual, String $message)	Reports an error identified by $message if the two variables $expected and $actual do not have the same type and value.
void assertNotSame(Object $expected, Object $actual)	Reports an error if the two variables $expected and $actual reference the same object.

Table 6. Assertions (continued)

Assertion	Description
void assertNotSame(Object $expected, Object $actual, String $message)	Reports an error identified by $message if the two variables $expected and $actual reference the same object.
void assertNotSame(Mixed $expected, Mixed $actual)	Reports an error if the two variables $expected and $actual have the same type and value.
void assertNotSame(Mixed $expected, Mixed $actual, String $message)	Reports an error identified by $message if the two variables $expected and $actual have the same type and value.
void assertEquals(Array $expected, Array $actual)	Reports an error if the two arrays $expected and $actual are not equal.
void assertEquals(Array $expected, Array $actual, String $message)	Reports an error identified by $message if the two arrays $expected and $actual are not equal.
void assertNotEquals(Array $expected, Array $actual)	Reports an error if the two arrays $expected and $actual are equal.
void assertNotEquals(Array $expected, Array $actual, String $message)	Reports an error identified by $message if the two arrays $expected and $actual are equal.
void assertEquals(Float $expected, Float $actual, Float $delta = 0)	Reports an error if the two floats $expected and $actual are not within $delta of each other.
void assertEquals(Float $expected, Float $actual, String $message, Float $delta = 0)	Reports an error identified by $message if the two floats $expected and $actual are not within $delta of each other.
void assertNotEquals(Float $expected, Float $actual, Float $delta = 0)	Reports an error if the two floats $expected and $actual are within $delta of each other.
void assertNotEquals(Float $expected, Float $actual, String $message, Float $delta = 0)	Reports an error identified by $message if the two floats $expected and $actual are within $delta of each other.
void assertEquals(String $expected, String $actual)	Reports an error if the two strings $expected and $actual are not equal. The error is reported as the delta between the two strings.

Table 6. Assertions (continued)

Assertion	Description
`void assertEquals(String $expected, String $actual, String $message)`	Reports an error identified by $message if the two strings $expected and $actual are not equal. The error is reported as the delta between the two strings.
`void assertNotEquals(String $expected, String $actual)`	Reports an error if the two strings $expected and $actual are equal.
`void assertNotEquals(String $expected, String $actual, String $message)`	Reports an error identified by $message if the two strings $expected and $actual are equal.
`void assertEquals(Mixed $expected, Mixed $actual)`	Reports an error if the two variables $expected and $actual are not equal.
`void assertEquals(Mixed $expected, Mixed $actual, String $message)`	Reports an error identified by $message if the two variables $expected and $actual are not equal.
`void assertNotEquals(Mixed $expected, Mixed $actual)`	Reports an error if the two variables $expected and $actual are equal.
`void assertNotEquals(Mixed $expected, Mixed $actual, String $message)`	Reports an error identified by $message if the two variables $expected and $actual are equal.
`void assertContains(Mixed $needle, Array $haystack)`	Reports an error if $needle is not an element of $haystack.
`void assertContains(Mixed $needle, Array $haystack, String $message)`	Reports an error identified by $message if $needle is not an element of $haystack.
`void assertNotContains(Mixed $needle, Array $haystack)`	Reports an error if $needle is an element of $haystack.
`void assertNotContains(Mixed $needle, Array $haystack, String $message)`	Reports an error identified by $message if $needle is an element of $haystack.
`void assertContains(Mixed $needle, Iterator $haystack)`	Reports an error if $needle is not an element of $haystack.
`void assertContains(Mixed $needle, Iterator $haystack, String $message)`	Reports an error identified by $message if $needle is not an element of $haystack.

Table 6. Assertions (continued)

Assertion	Description
void assertNotContains(Mixed $needle, Iterator $haystack)	Reports an error if $needle is an element of $haystack.
void assertNotContains(Mixed $needle, Iterator $haystack, String $message)	Reports an error identified by $message if $needle is an element of $haystack.
void assertRegExp(String $pattern, String $string)	Reports an error if $string does not match the regular expression $pattern.
void assertRegExp(String $pattern, String $string, String $message)	Reports an error identified by $message if $string does not match the regular expression $pattern.
void assertNotRegExp(String $pattern, String $string)	Reports an error if $string matches the regular expression $pattern.
void assertNotRegExp(String $pattern, String $string, String $message)	Reports an error identified by $message if $string matches the regular expression $pattern.
void assertType(String $expected, Mixed $actual)	Reports an error if the variable $actual is not of type $expected.
void assertType(String $expected, Mixed $actual, String $message)	Reports an error identified by $message if the variable $actual is not of type $expected.
void assertNotType(String $expected, Mixed $actual)	Reports an error if the variable $actual is of type $expected.
void assertNotType(String $expected, Mixed $actual, String $message)	Reports an error identified by $message if the variable $actual is of type $expected.

You may find that you need other assertions than these to compare objects specific to your project. Create your own Assert class to contain these assertions to simplify your tests.

Failing assertions all call a single bottleneck method, fail(String $message), which throws a PHPUnit2_Framework_AssertionFailedError. There is also a variant that takes no parameters. Call fail() explicitly when your test encounters an error. The test for an expected exception is an example. Table 7 lists the bottleneck methods in PHPUnit.

Table 7. Bottleneck methods

Method	Description
void fail( )	Reports an error.
void fail(String $message)	Reports an error identified by $message.

PHPUnit2_Framework_Test

PHPUnit2_Framework_Test is the generic interface used by all objects that can act as tests. Implementors may represent one or more tests. The two methods are shown in Table 8.

Table 8. Implementor methods

Method	Description
int countTestCases( )	Returns the number of tests.
void run(PHPUnit2_Framework_TestResult $result)	Runs the tests and report the results on $result.

PHPUnit2_Framework_TestCase and PHPUnit2_Framework_TestSuite are the two most prominent implementors of PHPUnit2_Framework_Test. You can implement PHPUnit2_Framework_Test yourself. The interface is kept small intentionally so it will be easy to implement.

PHPUnit2_Framework_TestCase

Your test-case classes will inherit from PHPUnit2_Framework_TestCase. Most of the time, you will run tests from automatically created test suites. In this case, each of your tests should be represented by a method named test* (by convention).

PHPUnit2_Framework_TestCase implements PHPUnit2_Framework_Test::countTestCases( ) so that it always returns 1. The implementation of PHPUnit2_Framework_Test::run(PHPUnit2_Framework_TestResult $result) in this class runs setUp( ), runs the test method, and then runs tearDown( ), reporting any exceptions to the PHPUnit2_Framework_TestResult.

Table 9 shows the external protocols implemented by PHPUnit2_Framework_TestCase.

Table 9. TestCase external protocols

Method	Description
__construct()	Creates a test case.
__construct(String $name)	Creates a named test case. Names are used to print the test case and often as the name of the test method to be run by reflection.
String getName()	Returns the name of the test case.
void setName($name)	Sets the name of the test case.
PHPUnit2_Framework_TestResult run(PHPUnit2_Framework_TestResult $result)	Runs the test case and reports the result in $result.
void runTest()	Overrides with a testing method if you do not want the testing method to be invoked by reflection.

There are two template methods—setUp() and tearDown()—you can override to create and dispose of the objects against which you are going to test. Table 10 shows these methods.

Table 10. Template methods

Method	Meaning
void setUp()	Overrides to create objects against which to test. Each test that runs will be run in its own test case, and setUp() will be called separately for each one.
void tearDown()	Overrides to dispose of objects no longer needed once the test has finished. In general, you only need to explicitly dispose of external resources (files or sockets, for example) in tearDown().

PHPUnit2_Framework_TestSuite

A PHPUnit2_Framework_TestSuite is a composite of PHPUnit2_Framework_Tests. At its simplest, it contains a group of test cases, all of which are run when the suite is run. Since it is a composite, however, a suite can contain suites that can contain suites and so on, making it easy to combine tests from various sources and run them together.

PHPUnit2_Framework_TestSuite contains protocols to create named or unnamed instances, as well as the PHPUnit2_Framework_Test protocols, run(PHPUnit2_Framework_TestResult $result) and countTestCases(). Table 11 shows the instance creation protocol for PHPUnit2_Framework_TestSuite.

Table 11. Creating named or unnamed instances

Method	Description
__construct()	Returns an empty test suite.
__construct(String $theClass)	Returns a test suite containing an instance of the class named $theClass for each method in the class named test*. If no class of name $theClass exists, an empty test suite named $theClass is returned.
__construct(String $theClass, String $name)	Returns a test suite named $name containing an instance of the class named $theClass for each method in the class named test*.
__construct(ReflectionClass $theClass)	Returns a test suite containing an instance of the class represented by $theClass for each method in the class named test*.
__construct(ReflectionClass $theClass, $name)	Returns a test suite named $name containing an instance of the class represented by $theClass for each method in the class named test*.
String getName()	Returns the name of the test suite.
void setName(String $name)	Sets the name of the test suite.

PHPUnit2_Framework_TestSuite also contains protocols for adding and retrieving PHPUnit2_Framework_Tests, as shown in Table 12.

Table 12. Protocols for adding and retrieving tests

Method	Description
void addTest(PHPUnit2_Framework_Test $test)	Adds $test to the suite.
void addTestFile(String $filename)	Adds the tests that are defined in the class(es) of a given source file to the suite.
void addTestFiles(Array $filenames)	Adds the tests that are defined in the classes of the given source files to the suite.
int testCount()	Returns the number of tests directly (not recursively) in this suite.
PHPUnit2_Framework_Test[ ] tests()	Returns the tests directly in this suite.
PHPUnit2_Framework_Test testAt(int $index)	Returns the test at the $index.

Example 21 shows how to create and run a test suite.

Example 21. Creating and running a test suite

```php
<?php
require_once 'PHPUnit2/Framework/TestSuite.php';

require_once 'ArrayTest.php';

// Create a test suite that contains the tests
// from the ArrayTest class.
$suite = new PHPUnit2_Framework_TestSuite('ArrayTest');

// Run the tests.
$suite->run();
?>
```

For an example of how to use PHPUnit2_Framework_TestSuite to compose test cases hierarchically, let's look at PHPUnit's own test suite.

Example 22 shows a cut-down version of *Tests/AllTests.php*; Example 23 shows a cut-down version of *Tests/Framework/AllTests.php*.

Example 22. The AllTests class

```php
<?php
if (!defined('PHPUnit2_MAIN_METHOD')) {
    define('PHPUnit2_MAIN_METHOD', 'AllTests::main');
}

require_once 'PHPUnit2/Framework/TestSuite.php';
require_once 'PHPUnit2/TextUI/TestRunner.php';

require_once 'Framework/AllTests.php';
// ...

class AllTests {
    public static function main() {
        PHPUnit2_TextUI_TestRunner::run(self::suite());
    }

    public static function suite() {
        $suite = new PHPUnit2_Framework_TestSuite('PHPUnit');

        $suite->addTest(Framework_AllTests::suite());
        // ...

        return $suite;
    }
}

if (PHPUnit2_MAIN_METHOD == 'AllTests::main') {
    AllTests::main();
}
?>
```

Example 23. The Framework_AllTests class

```php
<?php
if (!defined('PHPUnit2_MAIN_METHOD')) {
    define('PHPUnit2_MAIN_METHOD', 'Framework_AllTests::main');
}

require_once 'PHPUnit2/Framework/TestSuite.php';
require_once 'PHPUnit2/TextUI/TestRunner.php';
```

Example 23. The Framework_AllTests class (continued)

```php
require_once 'Framework/AssertTest.php';
// ...

class Framework_AllTests {
    public static function main() {
        PHPUnit2_TextUI_TestRunner::run(self::suite());
    }

    public static function suite() {
        $suite = new PHPUnit2_Framework_TestSuite('PHPUnit
                Framework');

        $suite->addTestSuite('Framework_AssertTest');
        // ...

        return $suite;
    }
}

if (PHPUnit2_MAIN_METHOD == 'Framework_AllTests::main') {
    Framework_AllTests::main();
}
?>
```

The Framework_AssertTest class is a standard test case that extends PHPUnit2_Framework_TestCase.

Running *Tests/AllTests.php* uses the TextUI test runner to run all tests, whereas running *Tests/Framework/AllTests.php* runs only the tests for the PHPUnit2_Framework_* classes.

PHPUnit2_Framework_TestResult

While you are running all these tests, you need somewhere to store the results: how many tests ran, which failed, and how long they took. PHPUnit2_Framework_TestResult collects results. A single PHPUnit2_Framework_TestResult is passed around the whole tree of tests; when a test runs or fails, the fact is noted in the PHPUnit2_Framework_TestResult. At the end of the run, PHPUnit2_Framework_TestResult contains a summary of all the tests.

This example shows the PHPUnit test suite running:

```
php AllTests.php
PHPUnit 2.3.0 by Sebastian Bergmann.

.........................................
.........................................
.......

Time: 4.642600

OK (89 tests)
```

PHPUnit2_Framework_TestResult is also a subject that can be observed by other objects wanting to report test progress. For example, a graphical test runner might observe the PHPUnit2_Framework_TestResult and update a progress bar every time a test starts.

Table 13 summarizes the external protocols of PHPUnit2_Framework_TestResult.

Table 13. TestResult external protocols

Method	Description
void addError(PHPUnit2_Framework_Test $test, Exception $e)	Records that running $test caused $e to be thrown unexpectedly.
void addFailure(PHPUnit2_Framework_Test $test, PHPUnit2_Framework_AssertionFailedError $e)	Records that running $test caused $e to be thrown unexpectedly.
PHPUnit2_Framework_TestFailure[ ] errors( )	Returns the errors recorded.
PHPUnit2_Framework_TestFailure[ ] failures( )	Returns the failures recorded.
PHPUnit2_Framework_TestFailure[ ] notImplemented( )	Returns the incomplete test cases recorded.
int errorCount( )	Returns the number of errors.
int failureCount( )	Returns the number of failures.
int notImplementedCount( )	Returns the number of incomplete test cases.

Table 13. TestResult external protocols (continued)

Method	Description
`int runCount( )`	Returns the total number of test cases run.
`Boolean wasSuccessful( )`	Returns whether or not all tests ran successfully.
`Boolean allCompletlyImplemented( )`	Returns whether or not all tests were completely implemented.
`void collectCodeCoverageInformation (Boolean $flag)`	Enables or disables the collection of code-coverage information.
`Array getCodeCoverageInformation( )`	Returns the code-coverage information collected.

If you want to register as an observer of a `PHPUnit2_ Framework_TestResult`, you need to implement `PHPUnit2_ Framework_TestListener`. To register, call `addListener( )`, as shown in Table 14.

Table 14. TestResult and TestListener

Method	Description
`void addListener(PHPUnit2_ Framework_TestListener $listener)`	Registers `$listener` to receive updates as results are recorded in the test result.
`void removeListener(PHPUnit2_ Framework_TestListener $listener)`	Unregisters `$listener` from receiving updates.

Table 15 shows the methods that test listeners implement; also see Example 26.

Table 15. TestListener callbacks

Method	Meaning
`void addError(PHPUnit2_ Framework_Test $test, Exception $e)`	`$test` has thrown `$e`.

Table 15. TestListener callbacks (continued)

Method	Meaning
void addFailure(PHPUnit2_Framework_Test $test, PHPUnit2_Framework_AssertionFailedError $e)	$test has failed an assertion, throwing a kind of PHPUnit2_Framework_AssertionFailedError.
void addIncompleteTest(PHPUnit2_Framework_Test $test, Exception $e)	$test is an incomplete test.
void startTestSuite(PHPUnit2_Framework_TestSuite $suite)	$suite is about to be run.
void endTestSuite(PHPUnit2_Framework_TestSuite $suite)	$suite has finished running.
void startTest(PHPUnit2_Framework_Test $test)	$test is about to be run.
void endTest(PHPUnit2_Framework_Test $test)	$test has finished running.

Package Structure

Many of the classes mentioned so far in this book come from PHPUnit2/Framework. Here are all the packages in PHPUnit:

PHPUnit2/Framework
   The basic classes in PHPUnit

PHPUnit2/Extensions
   Extensions to the PHPUnit framework

PHPUnit2/Runner
   Abstract support for running tests

PHPUnit2/TextUI
   The text-based test runner

PHPUnit2/Util
   Utility classes used by the other packages

Extending PHPUnit

PHPUnit can be extended in various ways to make the writing of tests easier and to customize the feedback you get from running them. Here are common starting points to extend PHPUnit.

Subclass PHPUnit2_Framework_TestCase

Write utility methods in an abstract subclass of PHPUnit2_Framework_TestCase and derive your test-case classes from that class. This is one of the easiest ways to extend PHPUnit.

Assert Classes

Write your own class with assertions specific to your purpose.

Subclass PHPUnit2_Extensions_TestDecorator

You can wrap test cases or test suites in a subclass of PHPUnit2_Extensions_TestDecorator, and use the Decorator design pattern to perform some actions before and after the test runs.

PHPUnit ships with two concrete test decorators. The first, PHPUnit2_Extensions_RepeatedTest, is used to run a test repeatedly and only count it as a success if all iterations are successful. The second, PHPUnit2_Extensions_TestSetup, was discussed in the section "Fixtures," earlier in this book.

Example 24 shows a cut-down version of the PHPUnit2_Extensions_RepeatedTest test decorator that illustrates how to write your own test decorators.

Example 24. The RepeatedTest Decorator

```php
<?php
require_once 'PHPUnit2/Extensions/TestDecorator.php';

class PHPUnit2_Extensions_RepeatedTest extends
    PHPUnit2_Extensions_TestDecorator {
    private $timesRepeat = 1;

    public function __construct(PHPUnit2_Framework_Test $test,
        $timesRepeat = 1) {
        parent::__construct($test);

        if (is_integer($timesRepeat) &&
            $timesRepeat >= 0) {
            $this->timesRepeat = $timesRepeat;
        }
    }

    public function countTestCases() {
        return $this->timesRepeat * $this->test->
            countTestCases();
    }

    public function run($result = NULL) {
        if ($result === NULL) {
            $result = $this->createResult();
        }

        for ($i = 0; $i < $this->timesRepeat && !$result->
            shouldStop(); $i++) {
            $this->test->run($result);
        }

        return $result;
    }
}
?>
```

Implement PHPUnit2_Framework_Test

The PHPUnit2_Framework_Test interface is narrow and easy to implement. You can write an implementation of PHPUnit2_Framework_Test that is simpler than PHPUnit2_Framework_TestCase and that runs *data-driven tests*, for instance.

Example 25 shows a data-driven test-case class that compares values from a file with Comma-Separated Values (CSV). Each line of such a file looks like foo;bar, where the first value is the one we expect and the second value is the actual one.

Example 25. A data-driven test

```php
<?php
require_once 'PHPUnit2/Framework/Assert.php';
require_once 'PHPUnit2/Framework/Test.php';
require_once 'PHPUnit2/Framework/TestResult.php';

class DataDrivenTest implements PHPUnit2_Framework_Test {
    const DATA_FILE = 'data.csv';

    public function __construct() {
        $this->lines = file(self::DATA_FILE);
    }

    public function countTestCases() {
        return sizeof($this->lines);
    }

    public function run($result = NULL) {
        if ($result === NULL) {
            $result = new PHPUnit2_Framework_TestResult;
        }

        $result->startTest($this);

        foreach ($this->lines as $line) {
            list($expected, $actual) = explode(';', $line);

            try {
```

Example 25. A data-driven test (continued)

```
                PHPUnit2_Framework_Assert::assertEquals(
                    trim($expected), trim($actual));
            }

            catch (PHPUnit2_Framework_ComparisonFailure $e) {
                $result->addFailure($this, $e);
            }

            catch (Exception $e) {
                $result->addError($this, $e);
            }
        }

        $result->endTest($this);

        return $result;
    }
}

$test   = new DataDrivenTest;
$result = $test->run();

$failures = $result->failures();
print $failures[0]->thrownException()->toString();
?>
expected: <foo> but was: <bar>
```

Subclass PHPUnit2_Framework_TestResult

By passing a special-purpose PHPUnit2_Framework_TestResult object to the run( ) method, you can change the way tests are run and what result data is collected.

Implement PHPUnit2_Framework_TestListener

You do not necessarily need to write a whole subclass of PHPUnit2_Framework_TestResult to customize it. Most of the time, it will suffice to implement a new PHPUnit2_Framework_TestListener (see Table 15) and attach it to the PHPUnit2_Framework_TestResult object, before running the tests.

Example 26 shows a simple implementation of the PHPUnit2_ Framework_TestListener interface.

Example 26. A simple test listener

```php
<?php
require_once 'PHPUnit2/Framework/TestListener.php';

class SimpleTestListener
implements PHPUnit2_Framework_TestListener {
  public function
  addError(PHPUnit2_Framework_Test $test, Exception $e) {
    printf(
      "Error while running test '%s'.\n",
      $test->getName()
    );
  }

  public function
  addFailure(PHPUnit2_Framework_Test $test,
             PHPUnit2_Framework_AssertionFailedError $e) {
    printf(
      "Test '%s' failed.\n",
      $test->getName()
    );
  }

  public function
  addIncompleteTest(PHPUnit2_Framework_Test $test,
                    Exception $e) {
    printf(
      "Test '%s' is incomplete.\n",
      $test->getName()
    );
  }

  public function startTest(PHPUnit2_Framework_Test $test) {
    printf(
      "Test '%s' started.\n",
      $test->getName()
    );
  }
```

Example 26. A simple test listener (continued)

```php
  public function endTest(PHPUnit2_Framework_Test $test) {
    printf(
      "Test '%s' ended.\n",
      $test->getName()
    );
  }

  public function
  startTestSuite(PHPUnit2_Framework_TestSuite $suite) {
    printf(
      "TestSuite '%s' started.\n",
      $suite->getName()
    );
  }

  public function
  endTestSuite(PHPUnit2_Framework_TestSuite $suite) {
    printf(
      "TestSuite '%s' ended.\n",
      $suite->getName()
    );
  }
}
?>
```

Example 27 shows how to run and observe a test suite.

Example 27. Running and observing a test suite

```php
<?php
require_once 'PHPUnit2/Framework/TestResult.php';
require_once 'PHPUnit2/Framework/TestSuite.php';

require_once 'ArrayTest.php';
require_once 'SimpleTestListener.php';

// Create a test suite that contains the tests
// from the ArrayTest class.
$suite = new PHPUnit2_Framework_TestSuite('ArrayTest');
```

Example 27. Running and observing a test suite (continued)

```
// Create a test result and attach a SimpleTestListener
// object as an observer to it.
$result = new PHPUnit2_Framework_TestResult;
$result->addListener(new SimpleTestListener);

// Run the tests.
$suite->run($result);
?>

TestSuite 'ArrayTest' started.
Test 'testNewArrayIsEmpty' started.
Test 'testNewArrayIsEmpty' ended.
Test 'testArrayContainsAnElement' started.
Test 'testArrayContainsAnElement' ended.
TestSuite 'ArrayTest' ended.
```

New Test Runner

If you need different feedback from the test execution, write your own test runner, interactive or not. The abstract PHPUnit2_Runner_BaseTestRunner class, which the PHPUnit2_TextUI_TestRunner class (the PHPUnit command-line test runner) inherits from, can be a starting point for this.

PHPUnit for PHP 4

There is a release series of PHPUnit that works with PHP 4 and does not require PHP 5. Due to PHP 4's limited object model, PHPUnit for PHP 4 is not a complete port of JUnit as PHPUnit for PHP 5 is. It also lacks certain features of PHPUnit for PHP 5, such as code-coverage analysis.

The PHPUnit release series for PHP 4 has its own PEAR package named *PHPUnit* (instead of *PHPUnit2*). This is because incompatible branches of PEAR packages (such as PHPUnit 1.X for PHP 4 and PHPUnit 2.X for PHP 5) have to be maintained in separate packages.

The following command line shows how to install PHPUnit for PHP 4 using the PEAR Installer:

```
$ pear install PHPUnit
```

A test-case class that is used with PHPUnit for PHP 4 is similar to one that is used with PHPUnit for PHP 5. The essential difference is that a PHP4 test class extends PHPUnit_TestCase (which itself extends PHPUnit_Assert, the class that provides the assertion methods).

Example 28 shows a version of the ArrayTest test case that can be used with PHPUnit for PHP 4.

Example 28. Writing a test case for PHPUnit 1.x

```php
<?php
require_once 'PHPUnit/TestCase.php';

class ArrayTest extends PHPUnit_TestCase {
    var $_fixture;

    function setUp() {
        $this->_fixture = Array();
    }

    function testNewArrayIsEmpty() {
        $this->assertEquals(0, sizeof($this->_fixture));
    }

    function testArrayContainsAnElement() {
        $this->_fixture[] = 'Element';
        $this->assertEquals(1, sizeof($this->_fixture));
    }
}
?>
```

PHPUnit for PHP 4 does not provide a TextUI test runner. The most commonly used way to run tests with PHPUnit for PHP 4 is to write a test suite and run it manually, as shown in Example 29.

Example 29. Running a test case with PHPUnit 1.x

```php
<?php
require_once 'ArrayTest.php';
require_once 'PHPUnit.php';

$suite  = new PHPUnit_TestSuite('ArrayTest');
$result = PHPUnit::run($suite);

print $result->toString();
?>
```

```
TestCase arraytest->testnewarrayisempty() passed
TestCase arraytest->testarraycontainsanelement() passed
```

Figure 8 shows the one feature that PHPUnit for PHP 4 has that PHPUnit for PHP 5 does not yet have: a test runner with a graphical user interface based on PHP-GTK.

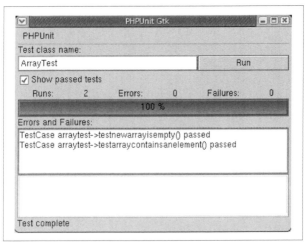

Figure 8. The PHP-GTK Test Runner

Bibliography

Astels, David. *Test-Driven Development: A Practical Guide.* Prentice Hall, 2003.

Beck, Kent. *JUnit Pocket Guide.* O'Reilly, 2004.

Beck, Kent. *Smalltalk Best Practice Patterns.* Prentice Hall, 2003.

Beck, Kent. *Test-Driven Development: By Example.* Addison Wesley, 2002.

Bergmann, Sebastian. *Professionelle Softwareentwicklung mit PHP 5.* dpunkt.verlag, 2005.

Gutman, Andi, Stig Bakken, and Derick Rethans. *PHP 5 Power Programming.* Prentice Hall, 2005.

Index

We'd like to hear your suggestions for improving our indexes. Send email to
index@oreilly.com.

Get even more for your money.

Join the O'Reilly Community, and register the O'Reilly books you own. It's free, and you'll get:

- $4.99 ebook upgrade offer
- 40% upgrade offer on O'Reilly print books
- Membership discounts on books and events
- Free lifetime updates to ebooks and videos
- Multiple ebook formats, DRM FREE
- Participation in the O'Reilly community
- Newsletters
- Account management
- 100% Satisfaction Guarantee

Registering your books is easy:
1. Go to: oreilly.com/go/register
2. Create an O'Reilly login.
3. Provide your address.
4. Register your books.

Note: English-language books only

To order books online:
oreilly.com/store

For questions about products or an order:
orders@oreilly.com

To sign up to get topic-specific email announcements and/or news about upcoming books, conferences, special offers, and new technologies:
elists@oreilly.com

For technical questions about book content:
booktech@oreilly.com

To submit new book proposals to our editors:
proposals@oreilly.com

O'Reilly books are available in multiple DRM-free ebook formats. For more information:
oreilly.com/ebooks

O'REILLY®

Spreading the knowledge of innovators   oreilly.com

©2010 O'Reilly Media, Inc. O'Reilly logo is a registered trademark of O'Reilly Media, Inc. 00000